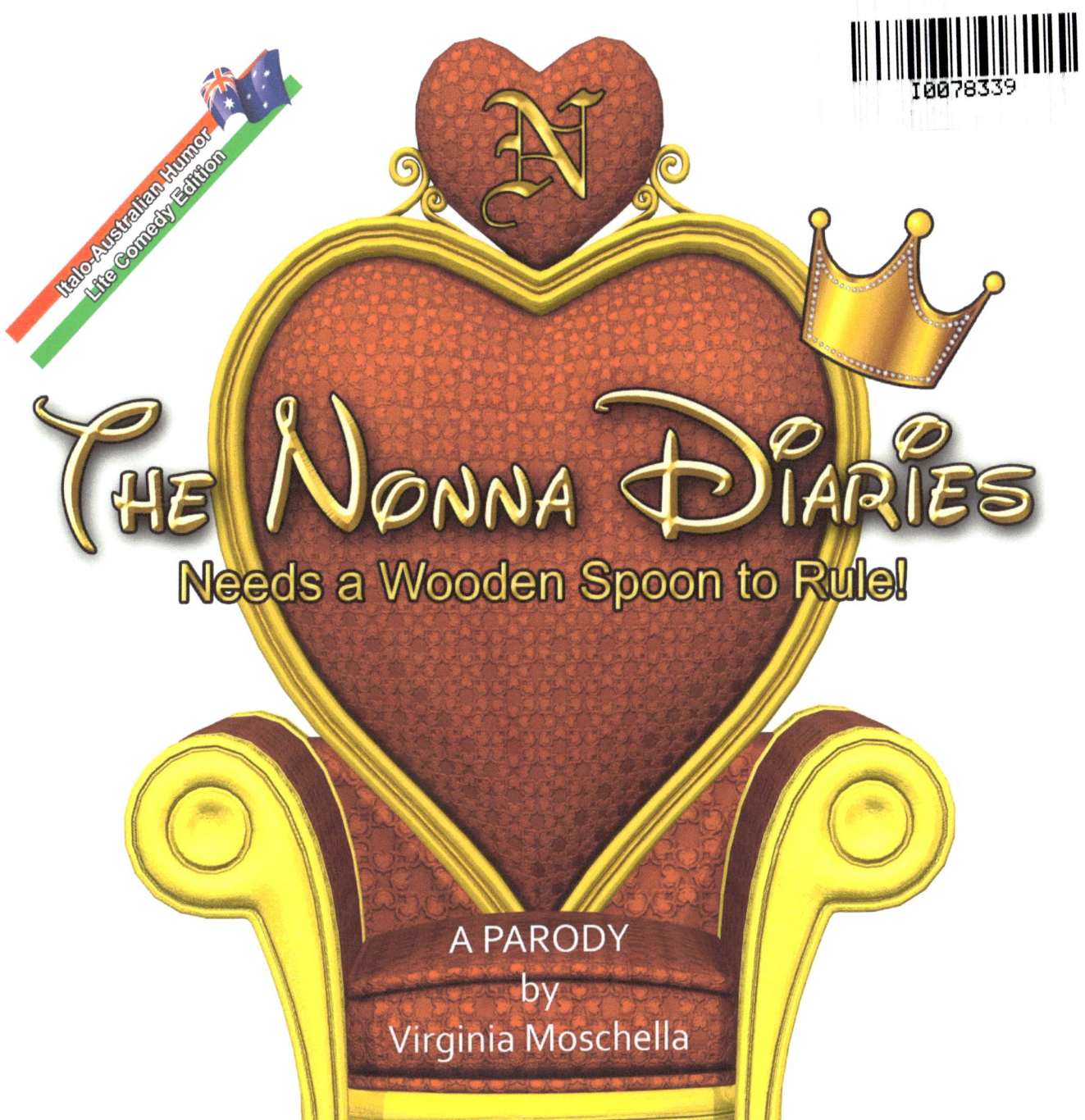

Copyright 2015 Virginia Moschella

All rights reserved in Australia, Asia Pacific Region, United States of America, Canada, Europe, United Kingdom. No part of this publication may be reproduced, stored electronically in a retrieval system, or transmitted through any means of electronic digital media formats through social media that includes recording, photographing, videography, photocopying, taping, graphic representation or otherwise, without the prior written permission of the publisher except when referenced in written and published book reviews or newspaper articles.

The opinions expressed in this book are purely written works that belong to the intellectual property of the author. Any reference or representation to people past and present have been used with discretion and will remain anonymous. Content is based on events that are factual and true with fictional characters. Dollarphoto club graphics - Stockphotos and Illustrations have been used for illustrative purposes only.
Published in Australia - Published Date 11/12/2015

GET THE E-BOOK SERIES ON AMAZON KINDLE

"GROWING UP ITALIAN AUSTRALIAN" - "I OWE MY LIFE TO SPAGHETTI"

All Correspondence to the Author -

Virginia MOSCHELLA

PO BOX 310   CAMPBELLTOWN SYDNEY

AUSTRALIA - NSW 2560

Email all inquiries to: moschellav@gmail.com

This book is dedicated to all
the beautiful Grandmothers all around the world!

ACKNOWLEDGMENTS

This book has been inspired from family and friends. There were many people who offered the author their own stories and unique experiences that contributed to the stories and funny moments treasured in their memories

CONTENTS

Author's Note   7

Chapter 1
Introduction   8

Chapter 2
My Big Italian- Mafia Wedding   10

Chapter 3
Driving with Mr Magoo   14

Chapter 4
The Lock Up Ages - The Italian Cinderella   20

Chapter 5
Nonna Calls Home   23

Chapter 6
Nonna's Fellowship of the Rings   28

Chapter 7
Gone Shopping!   33

Chapter 8
Nonna and the Bachelor   35

Chapter 9
Mafia Chef 'Cooking Just got even better'   38

Chapter 10
T'was the day of Christmas -
       Nonno Scrooge   44

Chapter 11
Dinner for Two at Nonna's Place   48

Chapter 12
Nonno and His Italian Cassettes   49

Chapter 13
Nonno Goes Fishing!   50

Chapter 14
More Nonni Jokes!   51

The End
"Good Bye, for now, until we meet again!"   56

Author's Note

You don't need to be crazy to be Italian, Nonna will train you! This is the second book in the series, 'Growing Up Italian Australian.' The daily conversations between Nonna and Nonno get even more interesting!

This is a parody, a lite comedy book about the trials and tribulations of growing up Italian Australian. It's so funny that you will keep on reading it over and over again. Just like a good tomato sauce, you will keep on coming back for more!

Chapter 1

Introduction

As migrants we were expected to give up our customs that set us apart from mainstream Australian society. All migrant's rights to maintain their own culture and language were only recognised in the 1970s with the advent of multiculturalism. Today we are a society of multi- races. Our Italian culture has a lot to say about who we are. Our growing up Italian Australian experience has shaped our characters and values. Yet we all have a sense of humour. Our relatives are our first extended family that we grow up with. No one understands our crazy *famiglia* like them! Now that we have all grown up, in every family, regardless of our heritage we all have some kind of special humour.

The book illustrates the experience of strange but true ways of our Italian-ess, *'sempre con respetto'* (always with respect) of course! Growing up Italian Australian, there are some things you need to know about our crazy generation; we suffer from severe sarcastic syndrome, especially when Nonna is unnerved. No one unnerves her like Nonno!

The stories illustrated in this book are based on fictional characters who are familiar to us all - our Nonni (Grandparents). The stories are all true believe it or not, with some fictitious characters just to maintain our incognito disguise. We are the Italian diplomatic community of course. Everyone loves an Italian and wants to be one too. As the Greek say, 'Una *facia una razzia*' (one face, one race). To the Italians we live by the rule..., "In Rome, do what the Romans do!" To the Australian, "She'll be right MATE!"

Chapter 2

My Big Italian- Mafia Wedding

It was 6 months to the date that we announced the *Matrimonio* (wedding). Over 350 invitations were sent out to all the relatives and friends that I didn't know. With only a week away from the big day, it was time to review the RSVP list.

Nonna was like a secret agent, who would do all her cold calls to check on the Comares and Compares, to see who hadn't sent back their RSVPs. Each day the postman came to our house, he was greeted by my pet Doberman 'Rambo'. The huge growl and the bark was the queue. Nonna would make sure she was there to receive the hand delivered mail. On this day we received 10 RSVPs.

Unopened, she would put the letters to the sunlight and see if the 'Yes' or 'No' box was ticked. If it was 'No' she would be so insulted that for days she would ask questions as to why?

Her remarks would be, "This Comare insults me! NO PANETONE this Christmas-a!" I remember the wedding ceremony and getting a 'boosta di soldi' (bundle of money, nothing less than $200) from the 350 guests who were invited. Then again I didn't even know most of them, however some were familiar as I had seen them at funerals. I suppose Nonna had to make sure that they were invited, if it wasn't a wedding invitation then the funeral would suffice at a later date. This was Nonna's way of making sure that no one was excluded, regardless of the event. At every wedding we danced to the tunes of favourite Sicilian folk village songs. I remember a song too well as a child, when we would dance and clap our hands, swing and do the twirls. We had so much fun growing up!

The Italian weddings were like a classic Sicilian scene in the Godfather movie. With the guests singing and dancing to the tunes that set the scene. The almond sugar confetti that were passed around, I would only eat the pink ones of course. The relatives, the parents of the bride and groom and then the bridal party with nothing less than twelve; six from the brides side and six from the grooms side. The obnoxious sister in-laws and in every Italian family was the 'black sheep', who we only knew of by name, but would not dare speak or gossip about them for respect of the family.

Then the stories of the Nonnas would emerge, as they tell of their own wedding back in the little villages of Sicily and Calabria. The hand embroidered dresses, the linen dowry that every bride was given and then the stories of the wedding night. This is where I blocked my ears, as I could no longer endure the visions of sugared confetti in my head with Nonna and Nonno on their wedding night. Enough was enough at this point. Photos were shared that showed a time of simplicity and joy. Black and white moments of history, like a frozen time capsule that dated 1949. The stories of our grandparents that have been past down to our generation are indeed treasured tales of an era that we will never understand.

Farewell to the telegrams from Italy and hand written letters. Familiar tunes would bring a tear to my eye whenever I heard these songs played at every wedding. Almost all the guests tend to cry towards the end when the Bride dances with their Papa (Father).

Especially the song 'Mamma and Parle Pui Piano' ('Mum' and 'Speak softly to Me') a classic Sicilian Godfather song, that was a bit confusing. My final Bridal waltz with my Father was a picture perfect moment. Guests were crying and so was my mother. It was a wedding not a funeral after all.

Chapter 3

Driving with Mr Magoo

I remember asking my Nonno, if I could borrow his car for a quick trip to the shops, as my car was getting repaired. It was like asking for blood! I thought I was going to send him to the hospital just for making a simple request. The answer by default was, "NO!" with a swear word thrown here and there, cursing even the heavens in blasphemy. I will not ever repeat these words for the love of God. I learnt very quickly to never ever ask him again. So instead Nonno would offer to drive me where I needed to go for the day. My own private chaperone, my own personal chauffeur and his name was, "Nonno MAGOO!"

To those of you who are too young to remember, I grew up watching a cartoon series called 'Mr Magoo'. A cartoon character that was created in 1949 and aired on television during the 60s-70s-80s as the 'Mr Magoo Show'.

The character was an elderly man who is wealthy. A retiree who gets into a lot of trouble in tricky situations whilst driving his little car. One would perceive him as a lunatic on the road as he has a problem with his eyesight while he is driving. My Nonno's problem was his blindness caused by his cataracts that prevented him from seeing the road ahead, and of course his Sicilian temper! Yes, my Nonno was also a lunatic on the road. Anyway, Mr Magoo's problem is his nearsightedness combined with stubbornness and will. My Nonno's problem was that there was none!

Everything that happened to him was a result of other people's misfortune and he was never to blame for their poor judgements in the situation. One day Nonno, has another car accident. Nonno is coming out of a side street when he collides with two cars. He was a bit shaken from the collision and so were the other two drivers. So he takes out his bottle of homemade wine. He says, "Here, have a taste of my wine?"

The other driver thanks him for the quick sip and then returns the favour and offers the wine back to him, "Here, you too?" Nonno graciously refuses the kind gesture and encourages him to drink as much as he wants, that he has plenty more at home. He sees the police approaching, covers his mouth and in a whisper says to the driver, "Oh, NO! thanks - it's OK, better wait until after the police come." Like a quiet assassin, Nonno walks away from the driver who was holding the wine bottle. Nonno pretends to complain about a limp in one leg while wiping the sweat from his forehead with his hanky as he hastily makes his quick escape from the car crash scene. He waits in the distance near his car that is parked on the side of the road for the arrival of the police. When the police arrive, all of a sudden my Nonno can't walk and complains of aches and pains in his left leg and that he has also hurt his head. This was an attempt to distract the policemen, while the other driver tried to hide the bottle of wine from view, he was caught in the act. "Nothing can save you now", thought Nonno as he watched the policemen approach the driver and question him about his wine bottle and the strong alcohol on his breath. The policeman asked him, "Sir, we would like to do a breath test on you?" The man agreed and to Nonno's delight he was over the limit and charged with drink driving. Nonno also agreed with the breath test, as it was only fair in the circumstances. When he was questioned about the accident, all of a sudden he couldn't speak a word nor understand English. How convenient I thought, and yet he got away with it as well. The ambulance arrived with the paramedics and Nonno thought that this was also an opportunity for a full physical examination to check his blood pressure, temperature and sugar levels. When he was given the all clear he was sent home.

On another occasion, Nonno and Nonna are on their way back home from visiting when they are stopped on their journey by the police. This time he is stopped for passing a red light. The policeman says, "Excuse me, I have to give you a fine for speeding over the limit and passing a red light." Nonna replies, "I told him to slow down and to stop at the red light." Nonno turned to Nonna and in broken English shouted, "SHUT-TA-UPPA!" The policeman not understanding what he said, asked Nonna, "Is that how he talks to you all the time?" Nonna nodding her head in embarrassment replies, "Only when he has drunk too much wine!" Nonno thanked the officer for the speeding ticket and the traffic infringement fine. Nonna said, "I hope he learns his lesson this time."

Later that week he receives a license renewal notice and a condition of his renewal is a routine eye test check at the Road and Traffic Authority office (RTA). Nonno was not too happy about this, and believed that the police officer who had fined him was responsible for this letter as it arrived at the same time with the fine reminder to pay notice. Reluctantly, he went to the RTA for the eye test and tried to convince the man at the counter that his vision was fine.

On his return I asked him how he went. He said he already went to the doctor. I replied, "That's good, so your eyes are good now? - But Nonno, which Doctor did you see? --- I thought you were going to the RTA?" Nonno hesitated for a while and there was a long pause and a slight twinkle in his eye when he replied, "Everything - all right-a!"

I replied, "Did you go to the eye specialist?" Nonno smiled at me and said, "Yeh... o'specialist-a at-ta RTA. He tell-a me to read A-B-C on the sign... but he try to trick me...he say to read the letters on the bottom. They were so small I couldn't see it...so I asked him to read it to me...I'm no stupido!" My Nonno not only failed the eye sight test but when he did the eye colour test, he was also colour blind as the traffic lights were green, white and red!

Never ask Nonno for driving advice. I remember when I went for my learner's driving test, Nonno 'Magoo' the expert driver decides to give me some advice. I asked him some questions that may help me understand the ethics of road rules and safety. So I asked him his thoughts about pedestrians crossing the road, "Nonno?...What do you do when you see a blind pedestrian crossing the road?" Nonno replied, "SFORTUNATO! he can't see your license plate! YOU keep on driving!" I was a bit taken back by that answer. So I asked him another question, "Nonno?... what about if there is a car that is passing you or you are trying to pass them?... Who should give way? - Me or the other car?" Now Nonno was smiling and acting quite proud about this response. He pointed to his eyes and said, "Keep eye contact always..., increase your speed quickly, and smile at the driver and say HALLO!...Thank You! as you drive pass. He has to give way to YOU 'cause you're the faster driver." I could not believe what I was hearing, my Nonno was not a law abiding citizen at all! So I said to him, "That's not good Nonno, you better not do that! You will lose your license!" Nonna also said, "That will serve him right!"

Chapter 4

The Lock Up Ages - The Italian Cinderella

Growing up Italian, at least we can say we survived the 'Lock up ages'- the 'Wrath of 100 death threats' and that was on a good day! The Italian girls went through the Cinderella era, cooking and cleaning with couch duties. Where was my fairy Godmother? After watching too many Godfather movies, the Sicilian curse was upon me. Nonna had her secret agents out and about town after school. At the gate she would wait patiently for our return home from school. Nonna would look so busy, pretending to water her roses and smile at the people who walked past to admire her garden, only to wet them accidently if she didn't like them. It would always be the ladies from the church group that she disliked or those who would steal her white roses. So she thought, that today was the day that she would teach them a lesson from the heavens.

She was attending to her rose garden when one of the church members past by her gate and pretended to not see her. She waits until she walks past the high brick fence and then showers her with the hose sprinkler. The lady let out a scream. Nonna peeks over the fence and says to her, "Looks like rain my dear, better bring an umbrella next time." That lady never walked past my Nonna's garden again. This would happen when ever I was coming home from school. It was so funny watching them look up to the blue clear sky for a rain cloud and see none. As soon as I arrived home, I would run inside to avoid any more attention and Nonna would follow looking over her shoulder if anyone had followed me home by chance. Looking very concerned with her googly eyes piercing through her thick brown glasses, she would take a quick glance at her watch, wondering where the hell my brothers were as they were on the same school bus. She would pace up and down the hallway until they arrived home safely. She was always concerned about our safely, making sure that we were home on time with an after school treat waiting for us as soon as we arrived home. However, on this day my brothers were running late, as they had after school football. Nonna was very impatient and started to worry about them. Suddenly to Nonna's surprise, a shadow appears behind the yellow stained class panel at the door. To her relief, or mine for that matter, there on the door step were her beloved grandsons. I would yell out from the kitchen, "Ah, the golden children have arrived! Nonna, you don't have to worry anymore!" As for me, it was straight to your room and get changed we have dinner to prepare. Nonna would ask my brothers, "Bello, what would you like to eat for dinner?" while she

pinched their chubby little cheeks (as if they weren't fat enough). He would reply, "Oh, Nonna! (gushing) we like the way you make spaghetti bolognaise." With a smile and a wink, she quickly put on her map of Sicily apron. It was back in the kitchen to cooking duties to cook up a storm of spaghetti bolognaise for the royal palace.

Chapter 5

Nonna Calls Home

Calling Nonna at home is like calling for the emergency telephone assistance. We have to call three times. The first call is to check that the phone works. The second call is to prompt her that the telephone is ringing and allow her time to get to the phone. The third call, if I'm lucky is when she picks up!

Anyway, Nonna still expects us to call her or drop by on a daily basis. If she hasn't heard from us in a while, let's say within 48 hours, then she expects us to call in on her to check up. So like a devoted and loyal servant, and most favoured grand-daughter, I ring Nonna on occasion to catch up on the neighbourhood gossip. I always call her three times, as the house phone is in the kitchen, and she is normally upstairs or in the garden and it takes her 30 minutes to get to the phone from where ever she is. Her hearing is also a bit of a miss, so hearing the phone ring is another aggravated problem to answering the phone.

So the three attempt rule applies. I let it ring three times, then hang up. Another three times, hang up again and then on the last attempt I am supposed to let it ring until she picks it up. She picks up every time on the third attempt. However, this time she doesn't and to my amazement I find out that Nonna has call waiting and I need to leave a message after the beep. So I try calling her again and leave another message and this time it gets transferred to Dad's mobile phone. Since when does Nonna not answer her house phone? Even on the mobile phone, it goes to voice message and then converted to text message. A while later my Dad calls me, and asks me to leave another voice message on Nonna's house phone cause she accidently deleted the message! "Why have a phone, just answer it!" I said, What's the difference!"

Finally, Nonna calls me back on my mobile phone, but gets my voice message instead as I was at work. So she tries again and again… but on the third call she decides to leave this message, "If you want to see Nonna ALIVE, call me back PLEASE!" Now, at this point I was a bit over it, calling her was like a game of cat and mouse trying to ring her and answer the phone. Eventually, we did make contact and what a relief that was. Even E.T. could phone home by using a makeshift communicator. Telecommunications was getting a bit too sophisticated for Nonna with all these satellites in space, getting an outer range single on my mobile phone didn't help me, and this raised other problems. So on her birthday, we all decided to buy Nonna the latest iphone to make it easy for her to call us anytime, anywhere. I showed her all the features of the iphone and how it works and explained to her that reception may be an issue if the bars are low. Just in case she needs to contact me, to check the bars for digital range of service. So what does she do? Like a lost terrestrial goes outside and points the iphone to the sky moving it about and checking the bar status for the best reception range. She discovers that to get a good connection she needs to stand somewhere between her bathroom window and the side garden gate.

One afternoon, she is in the garden with her iphone waving it about in the air and talking to it as if it was an imaginary friend. Like a secret government agent, I appear on the scene and hide behind the rose bushes to see what Nonna was up to in her secret garden. If only Spielberg could see me now.

The iphone was talking back to her and it was 'Suri.' She asked her about the weather and the chances of rain that afternoon and then pointed to the sky. Suri replied with such accuracy. Looks like Nonna and Suri had become good friends after all. At this point I was rather proud of Nonna as she had advanced in using technology. So I reveal myself and jump out behind the rose bush. I asked Nonna, what she was up to and Nonna replied that she wanted to check on the weather and see if it was going to rain, to which Suri then replied with a weather forecast on the possibility of rain.

To my surprise, I thought it was wonderful that Nonna was finally getting a grasp on technology, but Nonna went on to tell me that she and Suri had begun to experience a psychic connection with one another.

Every night, she recharges her iphone. She takes it into the kitchen, safely nestled in her apron like a baby. Standing by the power plug like an alien by the spaceship, she plugs in the iphone device to the charger. *Buona Notte Suri...Nonna is going to bed.*

Chapter 6

Nonna's Fellowship of the Rings

The fellowship of the Rings begins with the Sicilian Curse - L'Malocchio (derived from the Italian words for bad (male) and eye (occhio), known colloquially as *The Evil Eye*.

Anyone who has grown up Italian Australian , knows someone who knows all about it. Well you know what I mean! If you don't, let me tell you more. The general beliefs behind this absurd and strange tradition run through various cultures and religions from Ancient pagan civilisations that date back to the Ancient Romans. Envy being one of the evil sins, with symptoms that range from headaches, excessive stomach pains, and general malaise. I can see you nodding your head as this sounds familiar and it's just another day for some of us, but to the trained eye one can tell the difference.

In its more severe forms, the afflicted can end up bankrupt, ill, injured or even dead! According to Mr Ripley, Believe it or not many Sicilians and Calabrese today still practice the curse on their friends and relatives. The fellowship of all the Nonnas and their quest for the one golden ring (the wedding band) forged from 18ct Italian gold of course, to rule all other rings of power as the ultimate weapon in their campaign against l'Malocchio.

The curses date back to the days of the little village in Sicily. A village town no different to the suburbs where we live in today. The curses and the practice of spells range from region to region throughout southern Italy. Her chief allies are her Comares who all practice the pagan ritual amongst their family and friends.

Growing up Italian Australian, and in every Sicilian and Calabrese family there is one who has this one special 'Ring'. In my family fellowship it was Comare Gina, who is respected for having healing powers of the 'Ring'.

The story begins in the little village in Sicily, where Comare Gina grew up as a young girl. She learns about the powers of the 'Ring' from an old women in the village who is known as the village gypsy. She advises her that upon her marriage, she will be given a gold 'Ring', that this one 'Ring' has special powers that has many purposes that can heal, make predictions and if necessary cast spells on those who the 'Ring' dislikes.

So it happens to be, that Comare Gina gets married at the tender age of 18 and is given this one gold 'Ring' on her wedding day. She invests in her fellowship of the 'Ring' and begins her quest to seek out the powers. She works on a donation only, nothing less than $100 for a 30 minute session. She has built a nice double storey house , full-la brick-a with terrazzo marble floor. A castle amongst the suburbs (un castello) . She uses the power of her Italian 18ct gold wedding 'Ring' to take the Mal'occhio curse away at your request. No money back. That would be bad luck. So prepare yourself for the worst. I advise you to sprinkle some salt around the house from time to time to ward off the evil spirits.

Be aware of when you feel ill with symptoms of tummy aches or pains associated with headaches. Mumble a prayer with reference to the name of 'Sant'Antonino', a 'Hail Mary' or two and an 'Our Father' just in case, and in severe cases a 'Glory Be', which will take several minutes, and poof! it's gone just like that.

Other methods includes water, olive oil, and the 'Ring'. It all comes into play. It can solve a family mystery. This process is actually a lot of fun and quite easy even for the little Italian gypsy in you. It's more effective to perform these rituals during spiritual religious calendar events such as 'Good Friday', 'Christmas Eve' or even during the month of November 'All Souls' or on an eve of 'Halloween' to ward off the evil spirits .

Here are the step-by-step instructions

'Place water in a small dish and then drop olive oil slowly into it. If the olive oil disperses, the 'Evil Eye' is indeed present, and you pierce the oil with your fingers while reciting the prayers. You can also spin your gold ring from a string and watch it sway over the water.'

So now your armed against l'Malocchio. Who knows whether there's any truth to the superstition, but really, at this point who really cares! Til this day, my Nonna still participates in the monthly ritual. She smiles at her neighbours even the church ladies who she dislikes; sprinkles salt around her front door, along the footpath to the front gate and steps. Be always in possession of a plastic red pepper chilly horn charm on your key chain and dangle it from your rear view mirror in case of a car accident. This will help you to recover car crash expenses, as it is never your fault in any given situation, it's just the wrath of the curse remember.

Chapter 7

Gone Shopping!

"Basta! (BAH-stah!) Enough!...That's it!" I would hear this every time I would go to the deli on Saturday morning.

Nonna would yell over the counter to stop the deli man from putting too many olives on the scale. Basta, basta! Add it to the end of your order "Un kilo e menzo e basta!" Shout it to your visitors who would press the door bell one too many times, because it takes Nonna half an hour to answer the front door. "BASTA!" It was utter anarchy.

I remember going to the local butcher with Nonna. She would order 20 kilos of pork meat to make her salami and sausages. On this occasion the butcher over weighed her order and she yells out, "BASTA BASTA!" The butcher replied, "You BASTARD!" We quickly left the butcher without our order, never to return there again. Nonna made the quick exist through the door, leaving me behind to apologise for the misunderstanding.

My Nonna's English got her into a lot of trouble, and also it seems her attitude towards others was just as bad. On one occasion, we found ourselves in the pasta section in the local supermarket isle, when Nonna meets an Asian woman. Nonna told her at a supermarket that she should try and cut back on eating Chinese instant noodles and eat the local food instead. So she gave her a packet of spaghetti and tomato sauce.

Chapter 8

Nonna and the Bachelor

Nonna always tells me that as I grow older, I grow wiser. So when I see Nonna get all worked up over her favourite reality TV shows, my Australian TV realty show wisdom tells me, how ridiculous it is to get worked up over such meaningful entertainment.

Nonna watching 'The Bachelor' and 'Big Brother' was enough to send me over the edge. Nonna now gives special extra marital advice. Married twice, and twice divorced and now 'sex is legal' What is this all about? Nonna is not impressed. I remember getting married and Nonna giving me advice (all men should rejoice with her philosophy, it's woman's duty to get it on!) Oh! how I would cringe at what she literally meant in her Sicilian ways back in the day of her village adventures.

Well, things got a bit interesting when Nonna discovered reality TV with 'Sister Wives', 'Housewife Husbands', 'Farmer wants a Wife',…but it was the series 'The Bachelor', that really got Nonna all worked up.

Especially when she approached me with this question."You know, I was watching 'The Bachelor'... All these people looking for n-a boyfriend....His nice.. I think these peoples should come to my-a place. I tell them. All girls need three things to get-ta boyfriend." So here is Nonna's Top 3 Tips, 'How to Marry a Bachelor' - According to Nonna, "One... needs nice-a shoes - Two... nice-a hair, get-ta haircut-ta before and Three... nice BOOBs --- like Sophia Loren!" Heaven behold the feminist movement, I had to swallow my tongue when I said, "Eh...OK? Is that ALL?" Nonna was quick on the mark to end her speech with, " Don't-ta forget. A man no want-na girl-la friend-a, they looking for n-a wife, like this show...You see (pointing to the screen on the TV). Look at these GIRL-las...All nice-y nice and then she go all crazy crazy... Start yelling at other GIRL-las... Say I like-a holidays, I like champagne..Walk along the beach! This GIRL-las NO GOOD!... She's na stupida.. Stronza!.. She forget that he wants n-a wife, NOT na-rompe-le-palle! (aka- ball breaker). He wants to marry na-girl-la that cooks, cleans and SHUT-RUPPA !"

Nonna is not impressed with these girls at all! She concludes with this comment, "He look'in for na-wife not na- girl-la friend-a!"

Chapter 9

Mafia Chef 'Cooking Just got even better'

Since TV has gone digital, we can now watch all her favourite shows on YouTube, and even record them on Foxtel I-Q. However, I do realize how extremely silly it is, if not for its political incorrectness and a few painful puns; that makes fun at multiculturalism and the love and passion for the Italian fusion recipes, that so called celebrity chefs of non-Italian backgrounds claim their five minutes of fame.

So for political implications, it motivates me to express Nonna's thoughts about the media cooking broadcast empire and reality cooking TV shows, with a focus on Italian food of course. Basically, there is one premium cable TV station on at home 24/7 currently on air in Australia, we have the cooking station on Foxtel I-Q, 'Food Network'.

Believe me, she has seen them all, from the Indigenous cooking show to the Indian Curry in a flurry shows with their 1 minute rice dishes. It seems that everyone on TV wants to be a celebrity chef, and Nonna agrees that you should learn to cook your own food that is part of your culture. This would solve global starvation, according to Nonna only an Italian can cook like an Italian, and if you're not Italian, well... you just can't pretend to cook like one. Don't even think of having an argument over this, she will win hands down. Her blood starts to boil when these wanna-be- Italian-Chefs get it wrong, and if she hears Italian Fusion with ravioli and lemon grass then Nonna is not a happy camper.

Now, before all you Italians make a big fuss about Jamie Oliver and Gordon Ramsey, as fans don't get offended. Let me make it very Italian and clear that I'm not here to judge whether Jamie Oliver can cook or if Gordon Ramsey needs anger management therapy. Who am I to judge? - The food broadcast networks are created for pure entertainment and has become the standard norm in today's television programming experience. Nonna doesn't need to apologize for expressing her opinions.

With Jamie Oliver cooking in his backyard amongst the manure, parsley, basil and old wood oven fire, Nonno would have no problem - not that there is anything wrong with it. That's how the Sicilians cooked back in the days of the little village. It has just taken us only 100 years to realise it, according to Nonna that's why the food tastes beautiful!

Her favourite celebrity chef is Stefano Di Pieri in little Italy, Mildura. His Italian, so he has the Italian stamp of approval! She gets all excited when she sees him walking through the vineyards, riding his little bike even though he is just a little bit top heavy. He drops in on the local Italians to have a quick word in Italian. Good O' Compare Stefano, always happy and loves his Italian food! Spreading the Italian cheer with the local villagers.

Another cooking show that she loves to watch is called, 'MasterChef'. This is where Nonna becomes one of the judges, and things are a bit shockingly intense when she begins to critic the contestants who want to cook like a MasterChef or rather like a 'MafiaChef'. Can they handle the heat in the Kitchen? According to her, there can be only one. She provides truly mesmerizing insights into her methods on cutting an onion to boiling pasta.

She loves the big fat Judge, Matt Preston known as one of Australia's best food critics; this is Nonna's Idol. She gets all worked up when he comments on the food and has to agree with the verdict. Then there is Jamie Oliver's Cooking show. Another standard TV show that relies on a dumbed-down version of 'fish n' chips' or the 'fish finger' sandwich for those who can't cook a boil egg and burn water.

Just the other night, I was watching Jamie Oliver's 30 minute meals on TV with my Nonna. Nonna commented, "I don't like this man, tell-a me how to make my olives!... and he use too much olive oil....and-a - extra virgin-ee!!.. That's expensive oil to use in the fry pan!...stupid-oo complet-a-menti! And he tell me how to cook Italian?.... And he say its takes 30 minutes, SCHEMO!!! takes me 5 minuti." Nonna has a love hate relationship with Jamie Oliver. He was demonstrating how to cut onions without crying. Nonna says, "STUPIDO!.... you get someone else to do it. SCHEMO!" Then the commercials came on, presenting Jamie Oliver's non-stick cooking pans. So Nonna decided that this time, maybe Oliver got something right. Nonna said, "SCHEMO! of course it's NO STICK PAN, if You NO COOK with it!"

Nonna watching cooking shows is not good for her health. I think she better stick to watching the soap operas instead. Every time she is watching these TV shows, all you can hear is yelling from the lounge room. She would yell at the top of her voice at the television, "AH! Your gonna burn the sauce... That's too much water for the pasta! You forgot the salt!... put it in Now!...COME ON, WHAT ARE YOU WAITING FOR... YOU TALK TOO MUCH...WATCH THE STOVE!"

Nonna's favourite celebrity chef is Gordon Ramsey. She gets a kick out of how angry he gets. Looks like Nonna and Gordon Ramsey's 'F' word cooking show is enough to get the blood pumping, only that she calls it the 'Va Funcullo' Show! Maybe a special episode could include a take on one of his shows 'Hell's Kitchen, but when we translate it into Italian it sounds more dramatic - 'Cucina L'inferno'.

What about 'Kitchen Nightmares', with Nonna as the host on her own realty Italian TV show. She asks Gordon for some ingredients;

Nonna: "Go and get me two potatoes?"

Gordan Ramsey: "Ok, here you are, is that it?"

Nonna: " YOU BRING ME TWO POTATOS! (in an angry voice), how am I going to cook for all these people in the restaurant with TWO POTATOES!" -VA- FUNCULLO! Go back and get another TWO POTATOES!" Poor Ramsey is all confused.

So Gordon asks Nonna, "How much olive oil do I put in the pan, Nonna?"

Nonna's reply, "BASTA BASTA! VA FUNCULLO, RAMSEY!, you put too much!... SCHEMO! complet-a-menti.....it's not butter you know!" Just imagine the heat in Nonna's kitchen.

Knowing his reputation and his standard of language is no different to Nonnas, especially name calling and the 'F' word . In this kitchen nightmare, Nonna needs a wooden spoon to rule!

Chapter 10

T'was the day of Christmas - Nonno Scrooge

Christmas has finally come this year and Nonna and I were getting a head start to the day of festivities by setting up the long table on the back verander under the grape tree vine. We were expecting about twenty or at least we were, Nonna was cooking for an army just in case.

Nonno and Dad would make the tables out of doors and prop them on his trestle saw horses as a makeshift dinner table. All the chairs in the house including the garage and the old wooden broken chair from Nonno's shed were used, even though it was broken with half a leg! All Nonna's fine china was used and the silver all polished and every Bessemer pot and pan that you could imagine to cook with.

My Nonno would sit in his favorite lounge chair, reading the Italian *'La Fiamma'* newspaper and listen to his AM news radio tuned into the Italian station of course. He would scold my brothers who would run in and out of the back kitchen door, slamming it behind them.

My mum and I were slaving away at the old gas stove with four burners, today she has the chef deluxe model with eight burners! Cooking up a storm with a hurricane that followed to include every delectable dessert under the Aussie sun. How she ever came up with these meals on her Chef-4 -burner gas stove and oven was truly a miracle.

My Dad was in the back yard feeding his chickens, attending to the fig trees and ensuring that the nets were well secured so that the black sparrows wouldn't get in. Nonna had her favorite figs covered with an old used stocking. My brothers and all the neighbourhood friends were playing cricket and making a slip n' slide out of Dad's orange roll of cement working plastic, that he uses for his concrete form work. Nonna's Sunlight dish washing detergent came in handy, made the slip n' slide very slippery indeed. When lunch was served, you could hear the yell across the street to the next street corner. Yes, lunch was served and it was at our place! The Italians declared an eating feast like no other in the neighbourhood.

Within seconds, the table was crowded with every relative and friend that included the invited and non-invited. At Nonna's place there was enough to feed an army and provide a solution for national and global famine. No one was turned away. Nonna would serve the wine to everyone, dividing the glasses according to who was drinking. He would start with the men who got a full beer glass, then the women with half a whisky glass and the children all got a nip of the Sambucca glass. The vino worked its magic, as we were all laughing at Nonno's singing to the tunes of his out of tune violin to 'O'Sole Mio' or rather 'O' Dear Me'... I need another glass of wine!

Upon reflection, today as I see my own family and we reflect on these special times of my childhood, to an outside looking into this scene, what would come to mind is that we were simple and we made the best with what we had with very little. Growing up Italian Australian, we lived the Australian dream being raised in an Italian household where family was the most important element of our existence.

To the Italians, we had established the secret of becoming the Italo-Australians in the lucky country called Australia. This is the greatest gift that we can pass down to our children, the new generation - the Italian Australians.

Chapter 11

Dinner for Two at Nonna's Place

Every time my friends came over, my Nonna was always compelled to feed them. On this occasion I came home to find her entertaining a friend. This friend came over often and he enjoyed the plates of pasta that she dished out. After a while I couldn't contain my curiosity any longer, so I asked Nonna who this person was? She replied, "It's been about 2 months now, I just can't remember and I am embarrassed to ask him?"

Chapter 12

Nonno and His Italian cassettes

Angelina at la Pizzeria is a good old style 50's classic Italian English humour that my Nonni danced and laughed. We listened to these great classic songs. *"Eh, Compari!" by Julius La Rosa* was a classic! Nonno would sing and wet his whistle to this tune. *"AY ZEE ZONA A Saxophona, a coma zee zona a saxophona, TOOT TOOT TOOT TOOT a Saxophone.... a tippity tippity ta!"* What great memories! The song of their youth that I got to experience in the 70s and 80s.

Chapter 12

Nonno Goes Fishing!

Nonna calls the police to report that Nonno has gone missing. The police ask for a description. Nonna describes him as 170 cm tall, black wavy hair and has a sweet smile & very friendly. The police go knocking door to door to verify the report. One neighbor, tells the police, *"Don't believe her. His 165 cm tall, bald has a fat belly and unshaven with a frown on his face."*

The neighbor goes and asks Nonna why she gave the police that report. Nonna replies, *"Just because I reported him missing, doesn't mean I want him back!"* Meanwhile, Nonno returns from his fishing trip and sees the Police at his door step. The Police ask Nonna, *"Is this your husband?"* Nonna replies, *"NO! don't be silly. His the local fisherman!"*

Chapter 14

More Nonni Jokes!

Nonna weight training! *Uno- Due - Treeeee!* FORZA *'Invincible Nonna'*. Meanwhile back in the garage with the onset of the summer tomato season, Nonno delivers 1 tonne of the ripest tomatoes from the market with a swarm of fruit flies. 200 empty Victoria Bitter 750ml bottles were washed and boxed ready for bottling. It was summer, it was hot, it's tomato sauce time!

Headaches

Nonno comes home to be greeted at the door by Nonna. As he walked through the front door, Nonna turned to him and asked..,

Nonna: *"Headache?"* **Nonno:** *"No thanks I already have one!"*

Nonno and Astrophysics

Nonno was outside one evening observing the stars in the night sky. I asked Nonno, *"Do you know about the stars? We learned about stars at school Look! there's the milky way and you can see the southern cross with alpha centauri!"* Nonno replied: *"I know plenty of stars...Sophia Loren, Jerry Lewis, Dino Martino, Mar-a-lina Monroe"* I replied: *"But Nonno... Do you know what the milky way is? What the planets are made of? Do you know about Mars?"*

Nonno replied: *"Yeh... Chocolate!"*

Nonno and Darwin's Theory Evolution according to Nonno. First we evolved from the sea, then creatures on 4 legs, then we evolved into 2 legs, there were the apes, then the *Italians!*

The Bird and the Bees Nonna was telling my 5 year old son how babies are made. She began by saying, *"A baby is made when a man and a woman are in love, but before that, they turn the light out."*

Nonna and the Hare Kishna

Nonno was speaking to a Hare Krishna Monk who stopped her in the street to ask for a donation.

Hare Krishna Monk: *"Ah, excuse me... a donation please?"*

Nonna: *"Do you believe in heaven?"*

Hare Krishna Monk: *"Our God, Krishna will take us to Krishna heaven...that is what we believe madam."*

Nonna: *" That's NOT TRUE!..When you die you go to heaven, well us catholics go to heaven, I never heard about Krishna Heaven!"*

Hare Krishna Monk replied: *"What about everybody else madame?"*

Nonna: *"Everybody else goes to HELL...here is $2! go and get an express bus ticket!"*

Nonno walks into an Art Gallery

Nonno the 'Artist', was admiring a painting that was on the gallery wall.

Shop Assistant: *"Do you like the paintings, sir?"*

Nonno: *"AHH, YES... I like painting very much!"*

Shop Assistant: *"Oh, so your an artist? So what do you like to paint?"*

Nonno: *" I like to paint the kitchen door."*

Nonno and the Lotto Win

After 55 years playing the lotto, Nonno WINS the BIG ONE! He runs home to tell Nonna..,

Nonno: *"Eh!.... I won the Lotto! QUICK, pack your bags...quick?"*

Nonna: *"Are we going on a plane or by car?"*

Nonno: *"Who cares, pack your bags ...BYE and don't come back!*

Nonno and the Free Cup of Coffee

Nonno asks the local Barister for a coffee..,

Nonno: *"Eh!… How much for a short black espresso?"*

Barister: *"$3.50"*

Nonno: *"Eh!, too much...how much for a refill?"*

Barister: *"FREE Sir."*

Nonno: *"OK, I take that one thank you."*

Italian Scramble One evening I was playing scrabble with Nonna and Nonno. Nonna was complaining that Nonno was taking too long.

Nonno: *"Espetta..WAIT...I'm tinking!" (as he scratched his head)*

Nonna: *"We're playing scrammble not patienc-a!*

The Call from the Plumber

Nonna was waiting all day for her favorite plumber to arrive so he could fix her kitchen sink. She received a phone call..,

Plumber: *" Ah, sorry for the late notice, but I'm all tied up?"*

Nonna: *"I send my husband to untie you, he come now."*

The End

"Good Bye, for now, until we meet again!"

So if you have ever wondered what it's like to be part of an Italian family, especially my crazy one and let alone all the one's all around the world--- Well, you have come to the right place. Italians like everything big and that includes our family. So growing up in one has its ups and downs. I was lucky enough to have survived it and I bet you were too! All the stories that I have shared from my family and friends are endless with so many more to be revealed in the next edition.

"For everyone who grew up in an Italian family similar to mine, this one is for you. If you didn't, it doesn't matter... this is for everyone young and old! Every culture has their story to tell."

Nonna is a notable woman, whose wisdom and acute sarcasm will outwit any politician or president. In the next edition, **'I Owe My Life to Spaghetti',** she will continue to entertain you with her wooden spoon philosophy views on life.

We meet her son, Guido and his new love interest. Nonna also joins FACEBOOK which is a worry. We also catch up with Nonno in his backyard. Nonno knows the benefits of going green, but before examining the benefits, it is important for him to understand what going green means. Yeh, right! Try telling Nonno that green living refers to a way of life that contributes towards maintaining the natural ecological balance in the environment and preserving the planet! His solution about helping to maintain the ecological balance on the earth is to cause a global meltdown. You will not believe what he gets up to?

Read all about it, in the next edition to the

'Growing Up Italian Australian' series.

'I Owe My Life to Spaghetti'

Available as a paperback book and kindle e-book edition

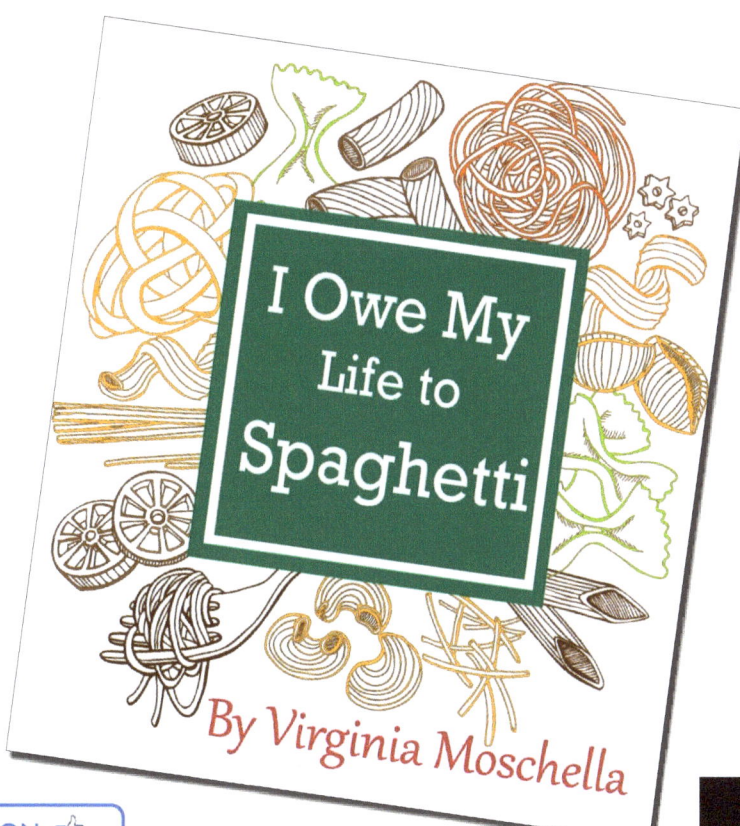

www.ingramcontent.com/pod-product-compliance
Lightning Source LLC
Chambersburg PA
CBHW060757090426
42736CB00002B/59